Southern Roots

Nurturing Debt Free Homestead Dreams

By

Linda Louise Lewis

Introduction

Welcome to the warm embrace of "Southern Roots: Nurturing Debt-Free Homestead Dreams," where we embark on a journey rooted in the timeless wisdom of Southern living. This guide isn't just about acquiring land; it's a celebration of the Southern way of life, entwined with the art of financial freedom and minimalism.

Everything I am going to guide you on in this book I have personally followed to obtain my debt free minimalistic lifestyle. I am confident that you can do the same, if you want it bad enough, dream of it night and day and put all of you into becoming debt free and a self-sufficient lifestyle and obtaining your on piece of land and homestead. It might take a while but it is well worth it if you work it with the same tenacity that you put into your favorite enjoyment in life!

My motivation in my endeavor was simple. Even if some kind of unexpected event happened and I had to start over, which seems to occur more often these days, I could still sleep on my own property and Good Lord willing...Start Over!

In other words, I had a place that no body was going to say I had this many days etc. to find another place to live or be homeless.

Chapter 1: Cultivating Financial Serenity

In the words of the wise, 'A penny saved is a penny earned.

Delving into the Traditional Southern Approach to Frugality and Financial Prudence:

In the heart of the Southern United States, a distinctive approach to frugality and financial prudence has been woven into the fabric of everyday life. Rooted in a culture that values hard work and resourcefulness, Southerners embrace a mindset that emphasizes the importance of making every dollar count. This traditional Southern approach to money matters embodies an old-timer horse sense philosophy that views wealth not just as a number on paper but as a reflection of one's values and character.

Southern wisdom dictates that financial prudence begins with a deep understanding of needs versus wants. It's about recognizing the difference between essential expenses and frivolous indulgences. Southerners often share tales of their elders, who were known for their ability to stretch a dollar and make thoughtful, intentional choices with their money. This approach fosters a sense of financial independence and self-reliance, echoing the sentiment that "money doesn't grow on trees" and must be earned with hard work and spent judiciously.

Unearthing the Unique Money-Saving Habits Ingrained in Southern Culture:

Southern culture boasts a wealth of unique money-saving habits that have stood the test of time. From the concept of "making do" with what you have to the art of preserving resources, Southerners have mastered the art of thriftiness. This often involves repurposing and reusing items, adhering to the belief that if something still has utility, it shouldn't be discarded.

Another cornerstone of Southern wisdom is the practice of homegrown sustainability. Many Southerners take pride in cultivating their own gardens, raising chickens, and engaging in other forms of self-sufficiency. This not only promotes a healthy and cost-effective lifestyle but also serves as a testament to the age-old wisdom that being financially responsible means being resourceful and finding ways to sustain oneself without unnecessary expenditures.

Actionable Step: Crafting Your Southern-Inspired Budgeting Plan:

Embracing the Southern-inspired philosophy on money matters involves translating traditional wisdom into actionable steps. Start by adopting a mindset of intentional living and budgeting. Craft a budget that reflects your values and priorities, distinguishing between needs and wants. Channel the spirit of Southern frugality by seeking out practical solutions, such as cooking at home, growing your own produce, and finding joy in simple pleasures.

Consider establishing an emergency fund, mirroring the Southern emphasis on preparedness for unforeseen circumstances. This echoes the old-timer horse sense philosophy of having "cash on the barrel" — a readiness to tackle financial challenges head-on without relying on credit or borrowed money.

Incorporate the Southern principle of community into your financial plan. Share resources, trade skills, and build a network of support. Just as Southerners have long understood the value of community ties, recognizing that collective strength can provide a safety net during tough times.

In conclusion, crafting a Southern-inspired budgeting plan involves more than just numbers; it's about embracing a mindset that values prudence, resourcefulness, and community. By weaving these principles into your financial practices, you can cultivate a sustainable and fulfilling approach to managing money, rooted in the timeless wisdom of the South.

Chapter 2: The Homestead Haven

As the magnolia blooms, so does the promise of a homestead haven.

Embracing Southern Soil

Understand the significance of land ownership in Southern culture.

In the sultry embrace of Southern winds, land isn't just dirt; it's the very soul of Southern living. It's where kinfolks gather, where stories are spun, and where traditions echo through generations. Your piece of earth isn't merely acreage; it's a legacy waiting to be written. Picture this: generations of your family, sipping sweet tea on a porch that your hands built — that's the heartbeat of Southern land ownership.

Explore the historical roots of Southern homesteading.

Back in the days when molasses flowed slow as molten sunshine, our forefathers carved homesteads into the land. Picture them, toiling under the Southern sun, building dreams from the ground up. Your journey begins where theirs left off, a proud torchbearer of Southern grit. Imagine the tales your homestead will tell – a living testament to the echoes of yesteryears.

Actionable Step: Set clear intentions for your homestead journey.

Now, darlin', grab a piece of paper and let the ink flow like a Mississippi riverboat. Outline your dreams, let them dance like fireflies in the moonlit Southern night. Set intentions so clear they cut through the fog like a hound dog's howl, guiding you to a homestead richer than red Georgia clay.

Finding Your Southern Sanctuary

Discover how to select the perfect Southern homestead location.

Close your eyes and imagine the perfect spot. Is it under the shade of a magnolia, or maybe nestled by a lazy, winding creek? The South is a mosaic of hidden gems; your job is to find the one that sings to your soul. Picture yourself standing there, feeling the pulse of the land, knowing it's where your roots will run deepest.

Uncover the secrets to evaluating land for homesteading potential.

Imagine you're in a sea of possibilities, each plot a canvas waiting for your strokes. But, sugar, not every piece of land is created equal. Learn the art of reading the lay of the land, like an old-timer reading the stars. Know where the sun kisses at dawn, where the shadows dance, and where the fertile secrets lie buried.

Actionable Step: Create a personalized checklist for choosing your homestead.

Craft your own roadmap, a checklist that's more sacred than a front porch swing at sunset. Picture it: your pen scratching off each requirement, a step closer to that plot of land that whispers, "This is home."

Southern-Style Tiny Living

Explore the charm and practicality of Southern tiny house living.

Think of a tiny house, not as cramped quarters, but as a love letter to simplicity. Picture your very own nest, cozy as a summer night, where every inch tells a story. Tiny living is an art, y'all – it's about embracing what truly matters and shedding the rest like Spanish moss from a cypress tree.

Learn how minimalism intertwines with Southern homesteading traditions.

Picture this: a kitchen where the scent of cornbread wafts through, a bedroom where dreams are woven into the quilts. It's not about less; it's about cherishing more. Minimalism isn't a sacrifice; it's a liberation, a hymn to the essentials that make life sweet as a Georgia peach.

Actionable Step: Plan and design your Southern-style tiny home.

Grab your sketch pad, envision the nooks and crannies that'll cradle your dreams. Plan a space where every beam echoes with your heartbeat, a tiny haven that's as big as the heart of Dixie.

Sustainable Southern Gardens

Dive into the art of cultivating a bountiful Southern homestead garden.

Imagine the symphony of cicadas as you stroll through rows of bounty – tomatoes plump as summer kisses, okra reaching for the sky. Your garden is more than plants; it's a Southern love affair with the earth. It's a dance of patience, sun, and rain, a choreography that yields not just sustenance but a taste of Southern magic.

Explore heirloom crops and sustainable gardening practices.

Imagine a tomato so juicy, it's a burst of Southern sunshine on your tongue. Heirlooms aren't just crops; they're stories, passed down like cherished tales. Learn the rhythms of the land, embrace sustainable practices that make your garden a haven for flora and fauna alike.

Actionable Step: Start your Southern garden with staple crops and herbs.

Get your hands in the soil, darlin'. Plant tomatoes that sing of summer, herbs that whisper secrets to the breeze. Picture your hands, seasoned by the Southern earth, nurturing life that'll grace your table like a feast from a Southern grandma's kitchen.

Homestead Harmony

Understand the holistic approach to Southern homesteading.

Think of your homestead not as pieces stitched together, but as a quilt, each patch complementing the other. Imagine the harmony – your garden, your tiny home, the land itself – a symphony of Southern living that resonates like a gospel choir on a Sunday morning.

Explore how different aspects of homesteading complement each other.

Picture it: a cycle where your garden feeds your family, your tiny home shelters your dreams, and the land cradles it all. See the interplay, the dance of elements harmonizing like a front porch fiddle and banjo duet. It's not just a homestead; it's a Southern serenade to life.

Actionable Step: Develop a comprehensive plan for your debt-free homestead.

Grab a mason jar, sweetheart, and fill it not just with sweet tea but with plans, dreams, and determination. Picture yourself debt-free, the weight lifted like a breeze through the Spanish moss. Craft a roadmap to a life where you owe nothing but gratitude to the Southern soil that cradles your dreams.

Chapter 3: Southern Strategies for Debt-Free Land Ownership

In the South, we say, 'If you want to own the land, you better understand the lay of it'.

Uncovering the Heartbeat of Southern Real Estate:

Embark on a journey to unveil the hidden gems and quirks of Southern real estate, where each plot of land whispers tales of history and possibility. Dive deep into the unique challenges that lace the landscape, painting a vivid picture of a region with its own set of rules and charms.

Southern Land Auctions and Bargains:

Step into the enchanting world of Southern land auctions, where whispers of opportunity flutter through the air like the rustle of magnolia leaves in the wind. Discover the art of negotiation, a dance as old as the southern traditions themselves, and learn to seize those hidden gems before they slip through your fingers like sand through a sweet tea sifter.

Example: Picture a quaint Southern town, where a charming parcel of land is up for grabs at an auction. As the sun sets on the horizon, bidding becomes a lively exchange, echoing the spirit of a barn dance. The savvy bidder, like a seasoned storyteller, weaves their way through the offers, leaving with a plot that's more than dirt—it's a piece of Southern soul.

Land Financing the Southern Way:

Explore financing options deeply rooted in the richness of Southern traditions, where handshakes carry the weight of a gentleman's agreement. Unearth the magic of owner financing and creative financial strategies that resonate with the sweet tea hospitality of the South.

Example: Imagine sitting on the porch of a rustic farmhouse, sipping sweet tea with a seller who's also your financier. In the Southern way, a deal isn't just about numbers; it's a pact made over shared stories and mutual respect. Your financing plan becomes a testament to the Southern charm, turning a transaction into a legacy.

Legal Labyrinths: Navigating Southern Land Laws:

Embark on a journey through the intricate maze of Southern land laws, where the path to acquisition is paved with the good intentions of a Southern drawl. Learn to waltz through the regulations, avoiding common pitfalls like a seasoned partner in a dance under the moonlight.

Example: Picture yourself at a crossroads, facing legal hurdles as thick as kudzu vines. A Southern-focused real estate attorney becomes your guide, not just through the paperwork but as a storyteller who decodes the legal tales that echo in the courthouses. The journey becomes a shared saga, where law meets lore.

Southern Roots: Cultivating a Strategy as Unique as Grits and Gravy:

Craft a real estate strategy with a dash of Southern flavor, where every decision is seasoned with the essence of magnolia blossoms and the rustle of live oaks. Your journey isn't just about transactions; it's a narrative that unfolds like a page-turner, with each chapter revealing the richness of Southern soil.

Example: Think of your strategy as a carefully tended garden. Just like a skilled gardener nurtures each bloom, your Southern-flavored strategy grows with care and attention. Maybe it's incorporating local festivals into your property marketing or embracing the charm of Southern hospitality in your dealings—whatever it is, let it be as authentic as biscuits from a grandma's kitchen.

Sweet Tea Serenity: Making Peace with Affordable Land:

Peel back the layers of Southern land searching, revealing the sweet center of finding affordable plots without sacrificing quality. Imagine your quest as a sweet tea expedition, where each sip brings you closer to the perfect blend of affordability and value.

Example: Picture yourself strolling through acres of open land, the scent of magnolias in the air. The journey isn't just about finding a plot; it's about savoring the process. Maybe it's discovering an overlooked gem—a pasture with a history that stretches back like the branches of a grand old oak. Your affordable find becomes a sweet victory, a sip of success in the Southern sun.

Magnolia Negotiation: Unveiling the Art of Southern Deal-Making:

In the dance of Southern real estate, negotiation is a waltz where each partner respects the other's rhythm. Unearth the secrets of magnolia negotiation, where the exchange of offers is a symphony and the closing is a grand finale that echoes through the moss-draped avenues.

Example: Envision yourself at the negotiation table, surrounded by magnolia blossoms. The art isn't just in the numbers; it's in the shared understanding. Perhaps you negotiate not just for a lower price, but for the inclusion of a porch swing, a symbol of Southern relaxation. The deal becomes a harmonious arrangement, a melody that resonates long after the papers are signed.

Front Porch Wisdom: Southern Sensibilities in Financing:

Delve into financing with the wisdom of a front porch sage, where terms are more than numbers—they're stories woven into the fabric of Southern sensibilities. Your financing plan becomes a tale of resilience, a narrative as enduring as the creak of a rocking chair on a lazy Sunday afternoon.

Example: Imagine sitting on the front porch with your financier, sharing dreams and aspirations. The financing isn't just a means to an end; it's a chapter in your story. Perhaps you negotiate terms that reflect the ebb and flow of life in the South—flexible and accommodating, like a slow river winding through the heart of the region.

Communal Hymns: Joint Land Ownership
Ventures:

In the South, land isn't just a possession; it's a
chorus, a collective hymn sung by a community.
Dive into the world of joint ownership, where
the beauty of shared dreams transforms the
real estate landscape into a communal
masterpiece.

Example: Envision a gathering where neighbors
become partners, and your venture into joint
ownership becomes a communal hymn. Each
owner contributes a verse, making the
ownership experience not just about division
but multiplication of joy. The land becomes a
canvas, painted with the diverse strokes of
shared aspirations.

As you navigate the labyrinth of Southern real
estate, let the spirit of the South guide you.

Each decision, each step, is a dance, a melody, and a communal experience. May your journey be as rich as Southern soil, as sweet as a summer evening on the porch, and as enduring as the stories passed down through generations of magnolia-scented whispers.

Southern Harmony: Orchestrating a Successful Land Auction:

Immerse yourself in the vibrant cadence of Southern land auctions, where every bid is a note in a lively tune. Picture yourself at the auction, surrounded by the energy of eager bidders and the thrill of uncovering hidden treasures. Your preparation isn't just about numbers; it's about understanding the rhythm of the auction and seizing the opportunity to conduct your own symphony of success.

Example: Imagine standing beneath a sprawling oak tree, the auctioneer's chant weaving through the air like a country melody. You've done your homework, recognizing the subtleties in the auction dance. As bids rise and fall like the rise and fall of a harmonious melody, you confidently join in, securing a piece of land that resonates with your vision. The auction becomes not just a transaction but a performance, with you as the maestro.

Legal Ballads: A Southern Attorney's Countryside Counsel:

Engage with a Southern-focused real estate attorney as if seeking the wisdom of a troubadour whose verses unravel the complexities of Southern land laws. Envision the attorney not just as a legal guide but as a storyteller, turning the legal labyrinth into a ballad where every clause has a verse and every regulation has a refrain.

Example: Picture yourself in a dimly lit office, the attorney's drawl adding a melodic touch to legal discussions. Like a troubadour sharing tales of yore, they guide you through the legal intricacies. It's not just about documents; it's about understanding the legal ballad, where pitfalls are like unexpected twists in a folk song. Your legal journey becomes a soulful rendition, complete with highs, lows, and a triumphant chorus.

Neighborly Bonds: Communal Collaborations Reimagined:

Extend a hand to your neighbors, not just as acquaintances but as fellow performers in the grand play of communal land ownership. Envision a gathering, where conversations about joint ventures are filled with laughter, shared dreams, and the spirit of a close-knit community. Your actionable step isn't just a transaction; it's an invitation to be part of a communal drama where everyone has a role and a stake in the outcome.

Example: Picture a community potluck, where discussions about shared land ventures blend seamlessly with the aroma of homemade pies. Your neighbors become co-authors of a story where the plot isn't just about property lines but shared aspirations. The land, once divided, now becomes a stage where everyone plays a part, turning ownership into a collective triumph.

In the grand narrative of Southern real estate, each element is a piece of a larger story. From the lively auctions to the legal ballads and communal harmonies, your journey is a symphony of Southern living. Let every decision be a stanza, every action a verse, and may the melody of Southern real estate guide you towards a harmonious and fulfilling venture, wrapped in the warmth of magnolia-scented dreams.

Soulful Landscapes: Crafting a Southern-Flavored Strategy:

In the enchanting tapestry of Southern real estate, your strategy is the brushstroke that paints the canvas of possibility. Imagine it as a quilt woven with the vibrant hues of Southern charm, stitched together with threads of hospitality and seasoned with the spice of local traditions. Your actionable step transcends mere planning; it's about infusing your approach with the essence of a front porch conversation, where every decision carries the soulful warmth of a Southern sunset.

Example: Envision yourself on a porch swing, mapping out your strategy like a seasoned storyteller. It's not just about numbers and timelines; it's about understanding the ebb and flow of Southern life. Perhaps your strategy involves aligning property showings with local festivals, tapping into the heartbeat of the community. Your journey isn't just transactional; it's a narrative woven into the very fabric of Southern living.

Southern Savvy: Unveiling Affordable Gems with Grace:

In the pursuit of affordable land, channel your inner Southern grace, where value is not just in the price tag but in the stories embedded in the soil. Picture your search as a leisurely stroll through a magnolia-lined avenue, each step revealing a new chapter in the narrative of possibility.

Example: Picture yourself exploring a hidden gem, an overlooked plot that whispers tales of bygone eras. Your search isn't about rushing; it's about savoring the journey. Maybe you uncover a piece of land that needs a little TLC, a diamond in the rough waiting to shine. Your find becomes not just affordable but a testament to your Southern savvy, recognizing the beauty beneath the surface.

Magnolia Magic: Negotiating with Southern Elegance:

As you enter the dance of negotiation, imagine it as a cotillion where each move is executed with Southern elegance. Your approach isn't just about haggling; it's about orchestrating a dance of mutual respect. Envision yourself at the negotiation table, where the art isn't in the cutthroat tactics but in the finesse of magnolia-scented diplomacy.

Example: Picture negotiations as a grand ball, where the terms are exchanged like a dance between partners. You gracefully navigate through offers, perhaps suggesting a compromise that includes not just a lower price but a commitment to preserving the heritage trees on the property. Your negotiation isn't just a transaction; it's a waltz of Southern charm, leaving both parties satisfied and enriched.

Blessings of the Front Porch: Tailoring a Southern Financing Plan:

Craft a financing plan that echoes the blessings of a front porch, where terms are agreed upon with the same sincerity as a Sunday sermon. Picture yourself sitting on that porch, rocking gently as you discuss financing, turning negotiations into a covenant sealed with the authenticity of a Southern handshake.

Example: Imagine the financing conversation not in a sterile office but on a porch swing, where terms are as comforting as the breeze. Your financier becomes a partner in the narrative, perhaps offering a flexible repayment schedule that aligns with the ebb and flow of the Southern seasons. Your financing plan becomes a chapter in your story, a testament to Southern sensibilities.

Chapter 4: Southern Homesteading Essentials

A Southern homestead is like a well-seasoned cast-iron skillet – practical, dependable, and passed down through generations.

Southern Kitchen Traditions:

Picture this: the aroma of biscuits baking in a cast-iron oven, the comforting sound of collard greens sizzling in bacon grease, and the laughter that fills the kitchen as stories are shared. In the South, the kitchen isn't just a place to cook; it's a sacred space where love is stirred into every pot.

As you tie on your apron, you're not just preparing a meal; you're crafting a symphony of flavors that speak the language of your heart.

It's about embracing the joy of simple, hearty, and budget-friendly recipes that echo the traditions of generations past. Want to dive headfirst into Southern living? Plan your week around meals made with affordable, locally sourced ingredients—because nothing says love like a pot of slow-cooked grits.

Southern Home Skills:

Now, let's talk about true Southern homemaking skills—the kind that involve more than just decorating. We're talking about mending fences, preserving peaches, and the art of making do. In the South, resourcefulness is a virtue, and fixing things up is a rite of passage.

Grab those overalls and identify three homesteading skills you want to master. Whether it's repairing a leaky roof or crafting homemade preserves, seek out local resources or classes to hone your craft. Remember, in the South, a well-mended fence makes for good neighbors.

Southern-Style Energy Independence:

It's time to cut those energy bills, y'all, and embrace a Southern-style energy revolution. Look beyond the utility companies and explore practical ways to harness the Southern sun and wind for your homestead. Imagine the satisfaction of watching your energy meter slow down as your homestead becomes a beacon of self-sufficiency.

Grab your toolbox and conduct an energy audit of your home. Plan for incorporating renewable energy sources, like installing solar panels or a wind turbine. In the South, the sun isn't just for sweet tea; it's for powering a homestead that stands strong against the changing tides.

Southern Water Wisdom:

In the South, we know the value of water—it's more precious than gold. Learn to manage water like a Southern farmer, collecting rainwater and practicing wise watering techniques. Make every drop count because, in the South, water is life.

Get your hands dirty as you set up a rain barrel, ensuring not a single drop goes to waste. Explore water conservation techniques that make you a steward of the land, because in a Southern homestead, we don't just grow crops; we nurture the very soil beneath our feet.

Homestead Healthcare, Southern Style:

When the sweet Southern breeze carries a hint of sniffles, it's time to turn to homestead healthcare. Dive into the world of natural remedies and create a basic homestead first aid kit. Picture this: a cup of chamomile tea for comfort, honey for healing, and aloe vera for soothing.

Start your medicinal herb garden, a treasure trove of remedies for those Southern sniffles. Imagine the satisfaction of crafting your own healing salves and teas, knowing that the remedy you seek is rooted in the very soil of your homestead.

Time to Put on Your Homesteading Overalls!

It's not just about growing veggies; it's about cultivating a way of life—a Southern way of life. Dust off that cast-iron skillet, grab your gardening gloves, and let's cultivate a homestead that's as hearty as cornbread and as sweet as peach cobbler. In the South, it's not just a lifestyle; it's a legacy, passed down through generations like a cherished family recipe. So, tie on those overalls, embrace the Southern breeze, and let's build a homestead that stands the test of time.

Southern Kitchen Traditions:

Picture this: the aroma of biscuits baking in a cast-iron oven, the comforting sound of collard greens sizzling in bacon grease, and the laughter that fills the kitchen as stories are shared. In the South, the kitchen isn't just a place to cook; it's a sacred space where love is stirred into every pot.

As you tie on your apron, you're not just preparing a meal; you're crafting a symphony of flavors that speak the language of your heart. It's about embracing the joy of simple, hearty, and budget-friendly recipes that echo the traditions of generations past. Want to dive headfirst into Southern living? Plan your week around meals made with affordable, locally sourced ingredients—because nothing says love like a pot of slow-cooked grits.

Southern Home Skills:

Now, let's talk about true Southern homemaking skills—the kind that involve more than just decorating. We're talking about mending fences, preserving peaches, and the art of making do. In the South, resourcefulness is a virtue, and fixing things up is a rite of passage.

Grab those overalls and identify three homesteading skills you want to master. Whether it's repairing a leaky roof or crafting homemade preserves, seek out local resources or classes to hone your craft. Remember, in the South, a well-mended fence makes for good neighbors.

Southern-Style Energy Independence:

It's time to cut those energy bills, y'all, and embrace a Southern-style energy revolution. Look beyond the utility companies and explore practical ways to harness the Southern sun and wind for your homestead.

Imagine the satisfaction of watching your energy meter slow down as your homestead becomes a beacon of self-sufficiency.

Grab your toolbox and conduct an energy audit of your home. Plan for incorporating renewable energy sources, like installing solar panels or a wind turbine. In the South, the sun isn't just for sweet tea; it's for powering a homestead that stands strong against the changing tides.

Southern Water Wisdom:

In the South, we know the value of water—it's more precious than gold. Learn to manage water like a Southern farmer, collecting rainwater and practicing wise watering techniques. Make every drop count because, in the South, water is life.

Get your hands dirty as you set up a rain barrel, ensuring not a single drop goes to waste. Explore water conservation techniques that make you a steward of the land, because in a Southern homestead, we don't just grow crops; we nurture the very soil beneath our feet.

Homestead Healthcare, Southern Style:

When the sweet Southern breeze carries a hint of sniffles, it's time to turn to homestead healthcare. Dive into the world of natural remedies and create a basic homestead first aid kit. Picture this: a cup of chamomile tea for comfort, honey for healing, and aloe vera for soothing.

Start your medicinal herb garden, a treasure trove of remedies for those Southern sniffles. Imagine the satisfaction of crafting your own healing salves and teas, knowing that the remedy you seek is rooted in the very soil of your homestead.

Time to Put on Your Homesteading Overalls!

It's not just about growing veggies; it's about cultivating a way of life—a Southern way of life. Dust off that cast-iron skillet, grab your gardening gloves, and let's cultivate a homestead that's as hearty as cornbread and as sweet as peach cobbler. In the South, it's not just a lifestyle; it's a legacy, passed down through generations like a cherished family recipe. So, tie on those overalls, embrace the Southern breeze, and let's build a homestead that stands the test of time.

Chapter 5: The Southern Mindset for Financial Freedom

In the South, we believe a clear mind and a full wallet make for a mighty fine pair.

Grab a seat on the porch; we're talking about the Southern art of mindful finance.

Imagine this, y'all. The sun setting over the magnolia trees, a gentle breeze kissing your face as you sit on the porch, sipping sweet tea. Now, let's talk about something as sweet as that tea – the Southern art of mindful finance. It's more than just numbers; it's about savoring every dollar and cent like it's a piece of your grandma's pecan pie.

Explore how mindfulness can lead to a debt-free life and a richer soul.

In the South, we believe in taking life slow and steady, just like a lazy river winding through the Georgia pines. Mindfulness ain't just about meditating; it's about tending to your financial garden with care. Picture this: by embracing the art of mindful finance, you're not just cutting debts; you're cultivating a richer, more fulfilled soul. It's the difference between rushing through life like a fast-paced rodeo and savoring the moments like a slow dance under a Southern moon.

Actionable Step: Start each day with a moment of financial mindfulness.

Picture this, darlin': sunrise over the cotton fields, a moment of quiet reflection. That's your cue to sip your coffee and set your intentions for the day. Take a breath, and think about your money goals – it's like setting a compass for your financial journey.

Generational Wealth Building, Southern-Style:

Down here, we don't just pass down sweet tea recipes; we pass down the secrets to building generational wealth. Think about Granny's cast iron skillet, seasoned over generations. That skillet didn't just fry chicken; it fried up financial wisdom that's been cooking in our families for ages.

Discover the art of creating a financial legacy that echoes through time.

Generational wealth is like a quilt stitched with the stories of our kin. It's not just about what you leave behind; it's about leaving a legacy that speaks of hard work, resilience, and the sweet taste of success. It's the difference between a fleeting dollar and a lasting heritage.

Actionable Step: Have a family meeting to discuss financial goals and legacy planning.

Gather 'round the dinner table, y'all. Pass the cornbread, and let's talk about more than just the weather. Lay out your financial dreams, share your goals, and let the wisdom flow from generation to generation like stories on a Southern front porch.

Southern Entrepreneurship and Side Hustles:

Put on your entrepreneur hat, sweetheart; we're about to turn Southern inspiration into profit. We ain't just making a living; we're making a life doing what we love. It's like turning those homemade jams into a thriving business – it's not just about the fruit; it's about the love and passion that goes into each jar.

Learn to make a living doing what you love.

Picture this: the smell of honeysuckle in the air as you work on your craft. Southern entrepreneurship is about turning your passion into profit, making your side hustle feel less like work and more like a dance under a starlit Southern sky.

Actionable Step: Identify a skill or hobby you can monetize and create a plan to launch your side hustle.

Whether it's pickling okra or crafting handmade candles, find what sets your soul on fire. Make a plan, like a recipe for success, and let your Southern charm shine through every venture.

Financial Freedom through Southern Community Engagement:

Community matters, sugar – it's the backbone of Southern living. We're talking about building a financial support network right in your backyard, where folks are as willing to lend a hand as they are a cup of sugar.

Discover how Southern communities come together to lift each other up financially.

In the South, when a neighbor's barn burns, we all bring the tools to rebuild. It's the same with finances – when times get tough, the community gathers, and we help each other rise like a batch of Grandma's buttermilk biscuits.

Actionable Step: Attend a local community event and start conversations about financial support.

Grab a plate at the church potluck, join in the country fair, and strike up conversations about dreams, struggles, and financial goals. Just like planting seeds in a community garden, you'll be cultivating connections that grow into a safety net when storms roll in.

Southern Philanthropy and Financial Freedom:

Down here, giving back ain't just a thing; it's a way of life. We believe in pouring a little extra sweetness into the tea of life. Philanthropy isn't just about writing a check; it's about making your money dance to a tune that echoes through your community.

Learn how contributing to your community can enhance your financial well-being.

Picture this: your dollars aren't just bills; they're seeds you plant in the community soil. As those seeds grow, so does your sense of purpose and prosperity. It's about realizing that financial freedom isn't a solo dance; it's a community square dance where everyone's steps contribute to a harmonious rhythm.

Actionable Step: Identify local causes or charities you'd like to support and make a plan for regular contributions.

Maybe it's the local animal shelter, the community center, or helping kids learn to read – find what pulls at your heartstrings, and commit to being a part of the solution. Like Granny's secret recipe, your philanthropy becomes a legacy that flavors the community for generations.

Time to Square Dance with Financial Freedom!

Clear the living room; we're about to square dance with financial freedom. From mindful mornings to building generational wealth, we're waltzing through the Southern mindset for financial freedom. So, put on your dancing shoes, and let's two-step our way to a debt-free, financially free life, y'all! Because, darling, financial freedom in the South ain't just about numbers; it's about dancing to the rhythm of a life well-lived.

Chapter 6: Southern Seasons of Financial Growth

Just like the magnolias bloom, our finances have their own Southern rhythm.

Spring: Planting the Seeds of Financial Success

As the azaleas bloom and the warmth of the Southern sun returns, we find ourselves in the season of financial rebirth – a time to plant the seeds of success that will flourish in the seasons to come.

Explore the Concept of Financial Spring:

Picture this: a field of wildflowers stretching as far as the eye can see. In the same way, your financial landscape is ready for a burst of color. This is your financial spring, where new opportunities bloom, and the air is filled with the promise of growth. We're not just talking about numbers on a page; we're talking about the dreams you've been longing to nurture.

Plant Those Financial Seeds:

Now, imagine you're planting seeds in this fertile ground. These seeds aren't just dollars; they're your aspirations, your goals. It's not about scattering them haphazardly; it's about placing them with care, tending to them like a cherished garden. What are your dreams? Owning a piece of land? Being debt-free? Starting a business? Plant those seeds and watch them sprout.

Actionable Step: Set Specific Financial Goals:

In the spirit of a Southern garden, set goals as diverse as a bed of daffodils. Want to pay off a credit card? Save for a down payment? Each goal is a seed waiting to bloom. Be specific, be intentional, and let these goals guide your financial journey through the blossoming seasons.

Summer: Cultivating Financial Abundance

With the hum of cicadas and the scent of magnolias in the air, it's time to bask in the financial sunshine – a season of abundance and growth.

Explore Strategies for Increasing Income:

Just as the Southern sun bathes the land in golden light, explore strategies that will bring more warmth to your financial picture. This isn't just about a paycheck; it's about finding ways to make your money work for you. Side hustles, investments, maybe even turning that passion project into a revenue stream – let the summer sun illuminate your financial landscape.

Make Hay While the Sun Shines on Your Financial Endeavors:

In the fields of finance, summer is your time to gather the hay. Imagine you're a farmer, diligently working under the sun to collect the abundance the land has provided. Similarly, seize the opportunities that summer affords. Don't just watch the sun; harness its energy to power your financial endeavors.

Actionable Step: Implement Income-Boosting Strategies:

Let your financial garden thrive. Implement income-boosting strategies tailored to your goals. Maybe it's negotiating a raise, exploring investment opportunities, or turning a hobby into a small business. Make hay while the financial sun is high.

Fall: Harvesting the Fruits of Financial Labor

As the leaves change colors and the air takes on a crisp edge, it's time to reap the rewards of your financial efforts – a season of harvest and celebration.

Explore Ways to Optimize Investments:

Picture a farmer surveying a field heavy with the bounty of a good harvest. Similarly, let's assess your financial landscape. Explore ways to optimize your investments, ensuring that each financial crop has flourished. This isn't just about numbers growing on a spreadsheet; it's about the tangible rewards of your labor.

Celebrate Financial Achievements:

Imagine a gathering under a Southern oak tree, where friends and family come together to celebrate the richness of the land. Your financial achievements deserve a celebration. Whether it's paying off a significant debt, reaching a savings milestone, or seeing returns on investments – celebrate these victories as you would a bountiful fall feast.

Actionable Step: Assess and Celebrate Your Financial Progress:

As you feel the weight of a well-earned pumpkin in your hands, assess and celebrate your financial progress. Take stock of your achievements, express gratitude for the abundance, and share the joy with those who have supported you.

Winter: Financial Hibernation and Planning

Winter isn't just a time for hibernation; it's a season of planning and building resilience against the financial chill.

Explore the Season of Financial Planning and Resilience:

Imagine a fireplace casting a warm glow in a cozy Southern home. This is the setting for your financial planning. Explore the season of resilience, where you not only weather financial downturns but also plan for the blossoms that lie ahead. This isn't about fear; it's about preparation.

Learn to Weather Financial Downturns:

Just as a Southern home is built to withstand both summer heat and winter chill, your financial plan should be resilient. Learn to weather financial downturns by fortifying your financial foundation. It's not about avoiding storms but about navigating them with confidence.

Actionable Step: Develop a Winter Financial Plan:

In the quiet of a winter night, develop a financial plan that will keep you warm through the season. Consider creating an emergency fund, reviewing insurance coverage, and identifying areas where you can trim expenses.

This plan is your financial fireplace, radiating warmth even in the coldest times.

Year-Round Financial Resilience

In the South, resilience isn't a seasonal affair; it's a year-round commitment. Your financial plan, like the evergreen magnolia, stays strong in every season.

Explore Strategies for Adapting to Financial Changes:

Picture a magnolia tree, its leaves glistening with dew in the early morning light. Similarly, explore strategies that keep your financial plan resilient. Adaptability is key. Whether faced with unexpected expenses, changes in income, or economic shifts, your financial plan should bend but not break.

Like the Evergreen Magnolia, Your Financial Plan Stays Strong:

The magnolia tree doesn't shed its leaves in the winter; it stays green and vibrant year-round. Similarly, your financial plan should endure. It's not about perfection; it's about persistence. Your goals may evolve, and challenges may arise, but your financial foundation remains steadfast.

Actionable Step: Create a Year-Round Financial Resilience Plan:

In the spirit of the magnolia, create a year-round financial resilience plan. Identify potential challenges, outline strategies for adaptation, and commit to nurturing your financial well-being in every season.

Time to Hoedown Through the Financial Seasons!

Grab your partner; it's time for a financial hoedown through the seasons. From planting seeds of financial success to harvesting the fruits of your labor, we're sowing the fields of financial abundance. So, dust off that straw hat, and let's dance through the financial seasons, Southern style!

Remember, this ain't just a dance; it's a journey. As you two-step through financial spring, waltz through summer's abundance, and square dance through fall's harvest, may your financial landscape be as rich and varied as a Southern quilt — a tapestry woven with dreams, resilience, and the sweet melodies of success. Now, let's hit the dance floor and celebrate your financial journey, y'all!

Chapter 7: Southern Sustainability Beyond Debt-Free Living

In the South, we don't just live sustainably; we do it with a touch of sweet tea and a side of cornbread.

Southern Sustainable Living Practices

In the Southern breeze that carries the scent of magnolias, sustainability isn't a trend; it's a way of life. Here in the South, we dance with the rhythm of nature, and it's time for you to join the Southern symphony of sustainable living.

Explore the Harmony Between Southern Living and Eco-Friendly Practices:

Imagine sitting on a porch swing, feeling the gentle breeze. That's the essence of Southern living, and it's harmonious with eco-friendly practices. We're not just talking about recycling bins; we're talking about weaving sustainability into the very fabric of your daily life. From the way you cook your grits to how you tend to your garden, every action becomes a note in the song of sustainability.

Learn to Make Sustainable Living a Part of Your Everyday Life:

Just as sweet tea is a staple on Southern tables, let sustainability become a staple in your life. It's not a distant concept; it's the choice you make when you brew your morning coffee or when you choose locally sourced veggies for dinner. It's about embracing a mindset where every choice aligns with the harmony of the Southern breeze.

Actionable Step: Implement One Sustainable Practice into Your Daily Routine:

Picture this: every morning, as you savor your cup of coffee, you take a moment to appreciate the beans sourced from a local roaster. That's your first step into Southern sustainable living. Your actionable step is simple – choose one sustainable practice, be it reducing single-use plastics or supporting local farmers, and make it a seamless part of your daily routine.

Sustainable Southern Agriculture

Down here, we don't just plant seeds; we cultivate a legacy in the soil. Our granddaddies taught us the art of farming, not just for today, but for generations to come. Now, it's time for you to step into the fields and embrace sustainable Southern agriculture.

Dive into Sustainable Agriculture Practices Rooted in Southern Traditions:

Imagine standing in a field of cotton, feeling the soft breeze and knowing that the land will yield not just this season but for years to come. That's the essence of Southern agriculture — a dance with the land that honors tradition. We're talking about crop rotation, cover cropping, and other age-old practices that keep the land fertile and singing with life.

Explore Regenerative Farming and Permaculture for a Sustainable Homestead:

In the Southern sun, we don't just farm; we regenerate. Explore the concept of regenerative farming and permaculture, where every plant and animal plays a role in the symphony of sustainability. It's not just about what you take from the land; it's about what you give back.

Actionable Step: Plan and Implement Sustainable Agriculture Practices on Your Property:

Imagine your backyard transformed into a patch of sustainable abundance — a place where chickens scratch, and vegetables thrive. Your actionable step is to plan and implement sustainable agriculture practices on your property. Whether it's starting a compost bin or integrating native plants, let your land tell a story of sustainability.

Southern Water Conservation Techniques

Water down here isn't just a resource; it's a legacy passed down through generations. Just as a Southern grandma guards her sweet tea recipe, we guard our water with respect. Let's explore the art of water conservation deeply rooted in Southern traditions.

Explore Traditional Southern Water Conservation Methods:

Picture a well-worn rain barrel catching the summer rain. That's the tradition of water conservation in the South – simple, effective, and handed down through the ages. We're talking about methods like rainwater harvesting and the wise use of irrigation. It's not about scarcity; it's about honoring the flow of water in the Southern landscape.

Learn How to Maximize Water Efficiency on Your Homestead:

In the Southern heat, water isn't just a necessity; it's a blessing. Learn the art of maximizing water efficiency on your homestead. It's about understanding the dance between the rain and your garden, using water wisely without letting a drop go to waste.

Actionable Step: Implement Water Conservation Techniques on Your Property:

Imagine a garden where every drop of water is cherished, where your plants flourish without excess. Your actionable step is to implement water conservation techniques on your property. Whether it's installing a drip irrigation system or capturing rainwater for your garden, let your homestead become a haven of water wisdom.

Energy Independence and Southern Sustainability

In the land where the sun kisses the earth with warmth and the wind whispers through the pines, it's time to harness the power of the Southern elements. Dive into the rich tradition of sustainable energy practices deeply ingrained in Southern living.

Explore Off-Grid Living and Renewable Energy Solutions:

Close your eyes and imagine a homestead where the hum of generators is replaced by the soft whir of wind turbines. That's the beauty of off-grid living, deeply rooted in Southern sustainability. Explore renewable energy solutions, from solar panels catching the

Southern sun to wind turbines harnessing the breeze.

Actionable Step: Take Steps Towards Achieving Energy Independence on Your Property:

Picture your homestead bathed in the soft glow of solar-powered lights. Your actionable step is to take tangible steps towards achieving energy independence. Whether it's installing solar panels or exploring energy-efficient appliances, let your homestead become a beacon of energy sustainability.

Sustainable Living Beyond the Homestead

Sustainability isn't just for your homestead; it's a gift you give to the entire community. In the South, we believe in influencing and contributing to sustainable initiatives that go beyond our property lines.

Actionable Step: Engage in Local Sustainability Projects and Organizations:

Imagine a town where every backyard is a small sanctuary of sustainability, and every street corner boasts a community garden. Your actionable step is to engage in local sustainability projects and organizations. Whether it's volunteering for a tree-planting initiative or supporting a community composting program, let your actions ripple through the town like a sweet Southern melody.

Time to Jig Through Southern Sustainability!

Put on your dancing shoes; we're jigging through Southern sustainability. From sustainable farming to water conservation, we're two-stepping towards a greener, more sustainable life. So, grab a partner, and let's dance through the fields of Southern sustainability together!

In this dance, your homestead becomes a stage, and every sustainable action is a step in a choreography of care for the land, the community, and the generations yet to come. Now, let's twirl through these sustainable practices with the spirit of a Southern celebration, y'all!

Chapter 8: Southern Legacy: Passing Down Debt-Free Homestead Dreams

In the South, we don't just pass down land; we pass down the stories written in its soil.

Generational Wealth: A Southern Tradition

In the heart of the South, where the magnolias bloom and the rivers whisper tales of old, there exists a tradition as enduring as the Georgia pines – the passing down of generational wealth. It's not just about money; it's about a legacy woven into the very fabric of Southern soil.

Explore the Southern Tradition of Passing Down Both Land and Financial Wisdom:

Close your eyes and imagine a porch bathed in the golden glow of the setting sun. Now, envision a grandparent passing the key to the homestead to the next generation. This is the Southern tradition of passing down both land and financial wisdom. It's a sacred ceremony where the stories of the land intertwine with the wisdom of the elders.

Learn the Art of Creating a Lasting Legacy for Future Generations:

Generational wealth is more than a bank balance; it's a narrative etched into the landscape. Explore the art of creating a lasting legacy for future generations. It's about planting seeds that grow into mighty oaks, providing shade for generations yet unborn. This isn't just about what you leave behind; it's about what you cultivate for those who will follow.

Actionable Step: Initiate Conversations About Generational Wealth with Your Family:

Imagine a Sunday supper where the aroma of biscuits mingles with the warmth of shared stories. Your actionable step is to initiate conversations about generational wealth with your family. It's not a lecture; it's a heartfelt discussion about dreams, values, and the responsibility of stewarding the Southern legacy. Share your vision for the future and listen to the dreams of those around the table.

Teaching Southern Financial Values

In the South, where the fireflies dance in the evening breeze, teaching financial values isn't a lecture; it's a conversation under the stars. It's time to instill the essence of Southern financial wisdom into the younger generation.

Understand How to Instill Southern Financial Values in the Younger Generation:

Think of a front porch, where the older folks share tales that carry lessons. Now, envision passing on financial values in the same manner. It's not about balance sheets; it's about weaving stories that teach the importance of frugality, hard work, and stewardship. It's the kind of financial education that doesn't come from textbooks but from the rich soil of Southern experience.

Explore Interactive and Engaging Ways to Teach Financial Responsibility:

Financial responsibility is learned not through lectures but through experiences. Explore interactive and engaging ways to teach financial responsibility. Picture a family garden where children learn to budget by managing the expenses of growing vegetables. It's hands-on, it's practical, and it's as Southern as a front porch swing.

Actionable Step: Create a Family Financial Education Plan:

Picture a calendar where financial education is as scheduled as Sunday supper. Your actionable step is to create a family financial education plan. It's not just about occasional talks; it's about regular, intentional discussions that involve everyone. From budgeting workshops to lessons about investments, let your family financial education plan be a roadmap to financial wisdom.

Family Homesteading Traditions

In the South, where the cicadas hum and the scent of honeysuckle fills the air, homesteading isn't just a lifestyle; it's a tradition passed down through generations. Let's delve into the art of creating lasting homesteading traditions within your family.

Delve into the Art of Creating Lasting Homesteading Traditions:

Picture a barn raising where neighbors come together to create something that lasts. Now, imagine the same spirit in your family, creating lasting homesteading traditions. It's about rituals like planting the first seeds of spring together or raising a handmade sign on the homestead's entrance. These traditions become the heartbeat of your family's homesteading journey.

Explore the Significance of Passing Down Practical Homesteading Skills:

Homesteading skills are not just practical; they are the threads that weave a family's homesteading tapestry. Explore the significance of passing down practical homesteading skills. Imagine a grandfather teaching his granddaughter how to mend a fence or a mother passing down the secret to a perfect biscuit. It's a legacy that transcends generations.

Actionable Step: Plan and Execute a Family Homesteading Tradition:

Picture a family gathering around a fire pit, celebrating a tradition that has been handed down through the years. Your actionable step is to plan and execute a family homesteading tradition. It could be an annual harvest feast, a tree-planting ceremony, or a day dedicated to crafting handmade tools. Let this tradition be a living testament to the resilience and unity of your homesteading family.

Nurturing Southern Values in Future Generations

In the South, where the hospitality flows as freely as the rivers, nurturing values isn't just a task; it's a way of life. Let's explore how to nurture broader Southern values and cultural heritage to pass down to future generations.

Explore the Broader Southern Values and Cultural Heritage to Pass Down:

Think of a front porch, where elders share stories that echo the values of the South. Now, imagine passing down those broader Southern values – hospitality, resilience, and respect for community. It's about teaching the kind of values that make a person not just successful but deeply rooted in the Southern spirit.

Learn How to Create an Environment That Fosters Southern Values in Children:

Values aren't taught in classrooms; they are absorbed from the atmosphere. Learn how to create an environment that fosters Southern values in children. Picture a home where every action, from sharing a meal to lending a helping hand, reflects the warmth and kindness that defines Southern hospitality.

Actionable Step: Identify Ways to Incorporate Southern Values into Your Family Life:

Imagine a home where the walls echo with laughter, and the scent of a home-cooked meal welcomes everyone. Your actionable step is to identify ways to incorporate Southern values into your family life. It's not about grand gestures; it's about small, consistent actions that become the building blocks of a Southern legacy.

Documenting Your Southern Legacy

In the South, where the live oaks tell tales and the rivers hold secrets, documenting your legacy is more than preserving memories; it's about passing down a story that echoes through time. Let's understand the importance of documenting your Southern legacy.

Understand the Importance of Documenting Your Southern Legacy:

Picture a well-worn journal filled with handwritten stories – that's the importance of documenting your Southern legacy. It's about preserving not just the facts but the emotions, the struggles, and the triumphs that define your family's journey. It's a living document that speaks to the hearts of future generations.

Explore Creative Ways to Preserve and Share Your Family's Story:

Preserving your legacy isn't about dusty photo albums; it's about weaving a tapestry that engages the senses. Explore creative ways to preserve and share your family's story. Imagine a family cookbook where each recipe is accompanied by a story of its origin or a video documentary that captures the essence of your homesteading journey. Let your creativity be the brush that paints the canvas of your legacy.

Actionable Step: Start a Family Legacy Project to Document Your Journey:

Picture a family gathered around a table, each member contributing to a project that immortalizes your story. Your actionable step is to start a family legacy project to document your journey. It could be a collaborative storytelling session, a scrapbooking weekend, or a digital archive where everyone contributes their part. Let this project be a living testament to the beauty and resilience of your Southern legacy.

Time to Waltz Through Southern Legacy!

The dance isn't over; it's time to waltz through your Southern legacy. From generational wealth to family traditions, we're twirling through the steps of passing down debt-free homestead dreams. So, grab your partner, and let's waltz into a future where your Southern legacy shines like a star on a clear Southern night!

In this dance, every conversation about generational wealth, every lesson in financial values, every homesteading tradition, every nurtured value, and every documented story becomes a step towards a legacy that doesn't just endure but flourishes like the dogwoods in spring. Now, let's waltz through these Southern legacy steps with the spirit of a grand Southern ballad, y'all!

Conclusion: Embracing the Sweet Symphony of Southern Living

As the last notes of the summer crickets weave through the warm Southern air, it's time to gather 'round the virtual porch and bid farewell to our shared journey through "Southern Roots: Nurturing Debt-Free Homestead Dreams." Y'all have become not just readers but fellow travelers in the tapestry of Southern living – from financial freedom to sustainable homesteading, and the rich legacy you're sowing in the very soil beneath your feet.

This guide ain't just a roadmap; it's the story we've spun together. So, kick off your boots, settle into your rocking chair, and let's reflect on the sweet symphony of Southern living that now reverberates through your very being.

Embrace the Essence of Southern Living:

Picture this: a front porch bathed in the golden glow of a setting sun, where the creak of the rocking chair is a lullaby and the fireflies dance like spirits from the past. You've not just embraced but embodied the essence of Southern living. It's not just about financial freedom; it's about the freedom to dance through life with the rhythm of the South.

Dance Through the Seasons of Financial Growth:

Think of your financial journey as a dance beneath the stars. You've learned the two-step of budgeting, the waltz of investing, and the jig of debt-free living. Now, as you sit on your porch, may your bank account reflect the harmony you've discovered. Remember, it's not just about numbers; it's about the sweet satisfaction of watching your dreams unfold.

Waltz Through the Homestead Essentials:

Close your eyes and envision a homestead where chickens cluck, vegetables thrive, and the scent of a freshly baked pie wafts through the air. You've waltzed through the homestead essentials, from sustainable agriculture to water conservation. Your homestead is not just a piece of land; it's a canvas where your dreams are painted in the hues of a Southern sunset.

Jig Through the Fields of Sustainability:

Now, imagine a field where wildflowers sway in the Southern breeze, and bees hum a melody of sustainability. You've jigged through the fields of sustainable living, from harnessing solar energy to engaging in local initiatives. Your commitment to sustainability is not just for you but a gift to the community and the generations that will follow.

Savor Every Step of the Journey:

In the South, we don't rush; we savor. Your journey ain't about reaching a destination; it's about relishing every step. As you look out onto your homestead, see it not just as a piece of land but as a testament to the love, hard work, and dreams you've poured into the Southern soil.

Share the Tales of Your Homestead Dreams:

Think of a summer evening where fireflies flicker like stars. Keep the porch light on, invite neighbors for sweet tea, and share the tales of your homestead dreams. Your story isn't just yours; it's a melody that adds to the grand Southern soirée of life.

Celebrate Life Like a Grand Southern Soirée:

Life in the South ain't just lived; it's celebrated. Picture a gathering under a canopy of magnolia trees, laughter echoing like a timeless ballad. Your homestead isn't just a piece of land; it's a stage for a grand Southern soirée. So, celebrate the bounty of the land, the joy of loved ones, and the sweet melody of a life well-lived.

May Your Homestead Dreams Be as Sweet as a Georgia Peach:

As you continue this Southern symphony, may your dreams be as sweet as a Georgia peach. Picture yourself walking through rows of peach trees, the fragrance enveloping you like a warm embrace. Your dreams are the fruits of your labor, and just like those peaches, may they be sweet, abundant, and shared with those you love.

Y'all Take Care Now:

As the Southern night unfolds with a blanket of stars, it's time to bid adieu. Y'all take care now, with the assurance that your journey is not just a guide's end but the beginning of a Southern story that unfolds with every sunrise. May your homestead dreams continue to flourish, and may the sweet symphony of Southern living play on in your hearts.

So, go on, darlin', dance through the seasons, cultivate your homestead haven, and pass down the wisdom like a cherished family recipe. The sweet symphony of Southern living awaits you.

Y'all take care now, and may your homestead dreams always be as sweet as a Georgia peach!

Linda Louise Lewis